AF599321

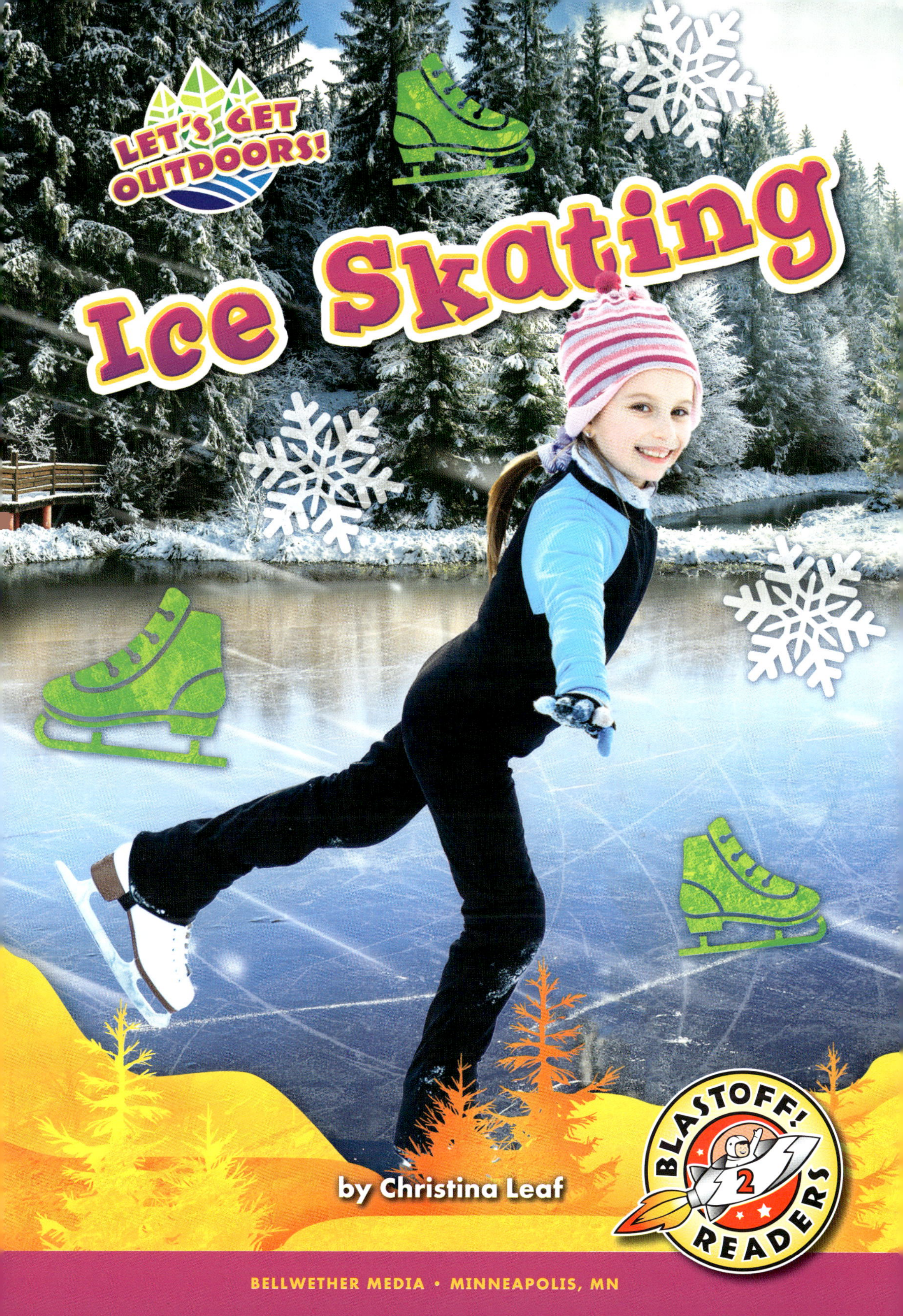
LET'S GET OUTDOORS!
Ice Skating
by Christina Leaf
BLASTOFF! READERS 2
BELLWETHER MEDIA • MINNEAPOLIS, MN

Blastoff! Readers are carefully developed by literacy experts to build reading stamina and move students toward fluency by combining standards-based content with developmentally appropriate text.

Level 1 provides the most support through repetition of high-frequency words, light text, predictable sentence patterns, and strong visual support.

Level 2 offers early readers a bit more challenge through varied sentences, increased text load, and text-supportive special features.

Level 3 advances early-fluent readers toward fluency through increased text load, less reliance on photos, advancing concepts, longer sentences, and more complex special features.

★ **Blastoff! Universe**

Reading Level

Grade K

Grades 1–3

Grade 4

This edition first published in 2024 by Bellwether Media, Inc.

Library of Congress Cataloging-in-Publication Data

Names: Leaf, Christina, author.
Title: Ice skating / by Christina Leaf.
Description: Minneapolis, MN : Bellwether Media, 2024. | Series: Blastoff! readers. Let's get outdoors! | Includes bibliographical references and index. | Audience: Ages 5-8 | Audience: Grades 2-3 | Summary: "Relevant images match informative text in this introduction to ice skating. Intended for students in kindergarten through third grade"– Provided by publisher.
Identifiers: LCCN 2023035123 (print) | LCCN 2023035124 (ebook) | ISBN 9798886878004 (library binding) | ISBN 9798886878943 (ebook)
Subjects: LCSH: Skating–Juvenile literature.
Classification: LCC GV849 .L39 2024 (print) | LCC GV849 (ebook) | DDC 796.91–dc23/eng/20230804
LC record available at https://lccn.loc.gov/2023035123
LC ebook record available at https://lccn.loc.gov/2023035124

Editor: Elizabeth Neuenfeldt Series Design: Andrea Schneider Book Designer: Josh Brink

Printed in the United States of America, North Mankato, MN.

Table of Contents

What Is Ice Skating?

Ice skating is **gliding** over ice on ice skates. Ice skates have sharp blades on the bottom.

Many people ice skate for exercise. People also ice skate for fun!

Many people skate at **ice rinks**. They can be inside or outside.

Others skate on lakes or ponds.

Lake Louise, Alberta, Canada

Claim to Fame

- located in Banff National Park
- features an ice castle and ice rinks

On the Ice

Skaters push off on one foot. They glide. Then they push off on their other foot.

It can take time to learn to **balance**!

There are many ways to ice skate. Some people **figure skate**. They do spins and jumps.

figure skating

playing hockey

stick

puck

Some people play hockey with sticks and a **puck**. Others may **speed skate**.

Ice Skating Gear

Different activities use different skates. Figure skates have **toe picks**. They help with tricks!

Hockey skates have hard shells to protect feet. Speed skates have long blades.

Types of Ice Skates

figure skates

hockey skates

speed skates

Ice skates are the main gear needed to ice skate. Beginners wear helmets.

Coats keep skaters warm. Hats and gloves do, too!

Skaters on frozen lakes must be prepared.

They should take life jackets, ropes, and cell phones. They safely carry **ice picks**.

Ice Skating Safety

Skaters on lakes and ponds must make sure the ice is safe. Thin ice is dangerous.

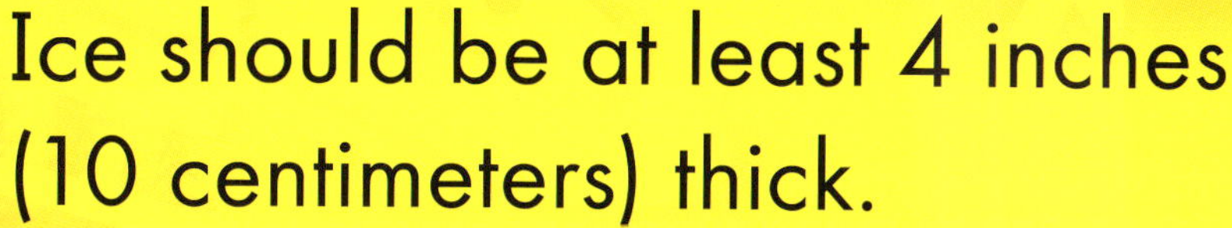

Ice should be at least 4 inches (10 centimeters) thick.

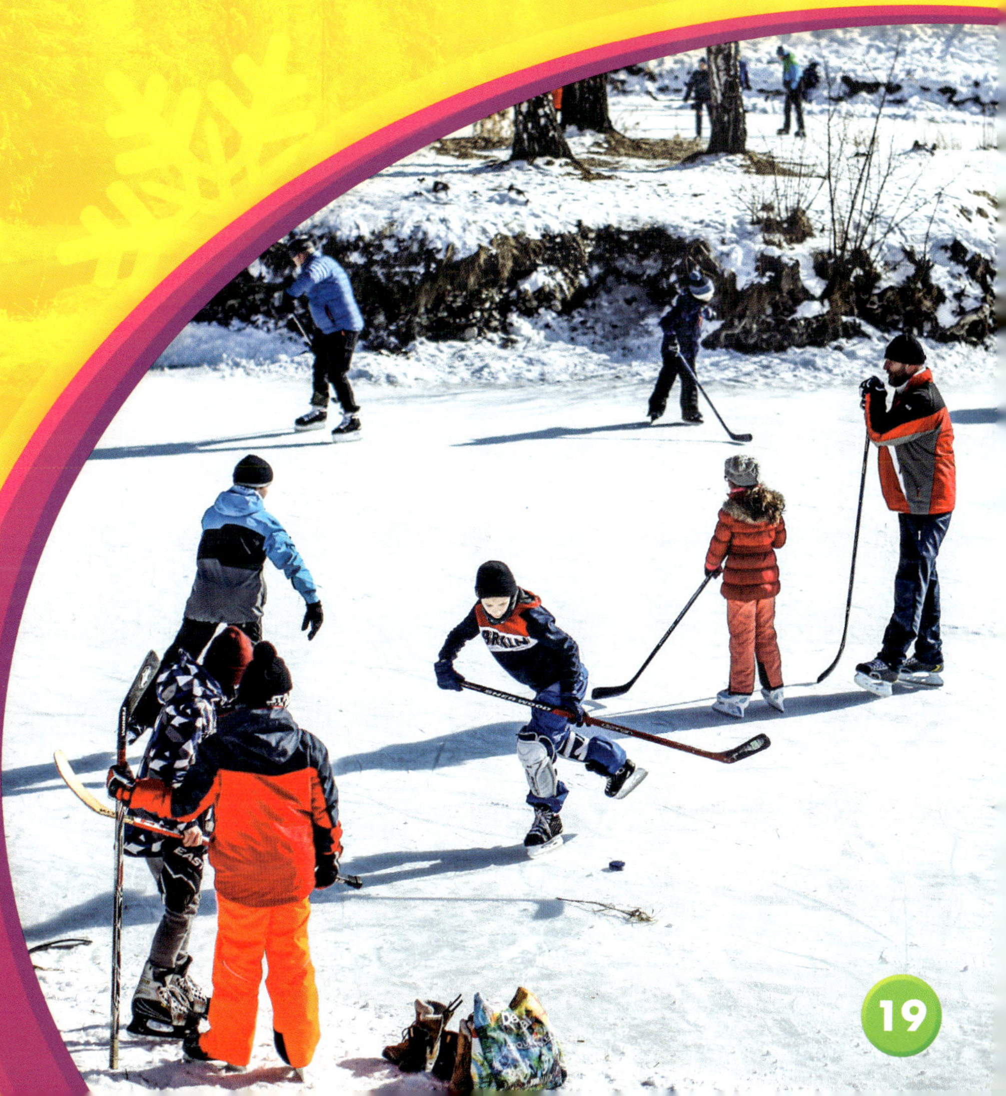

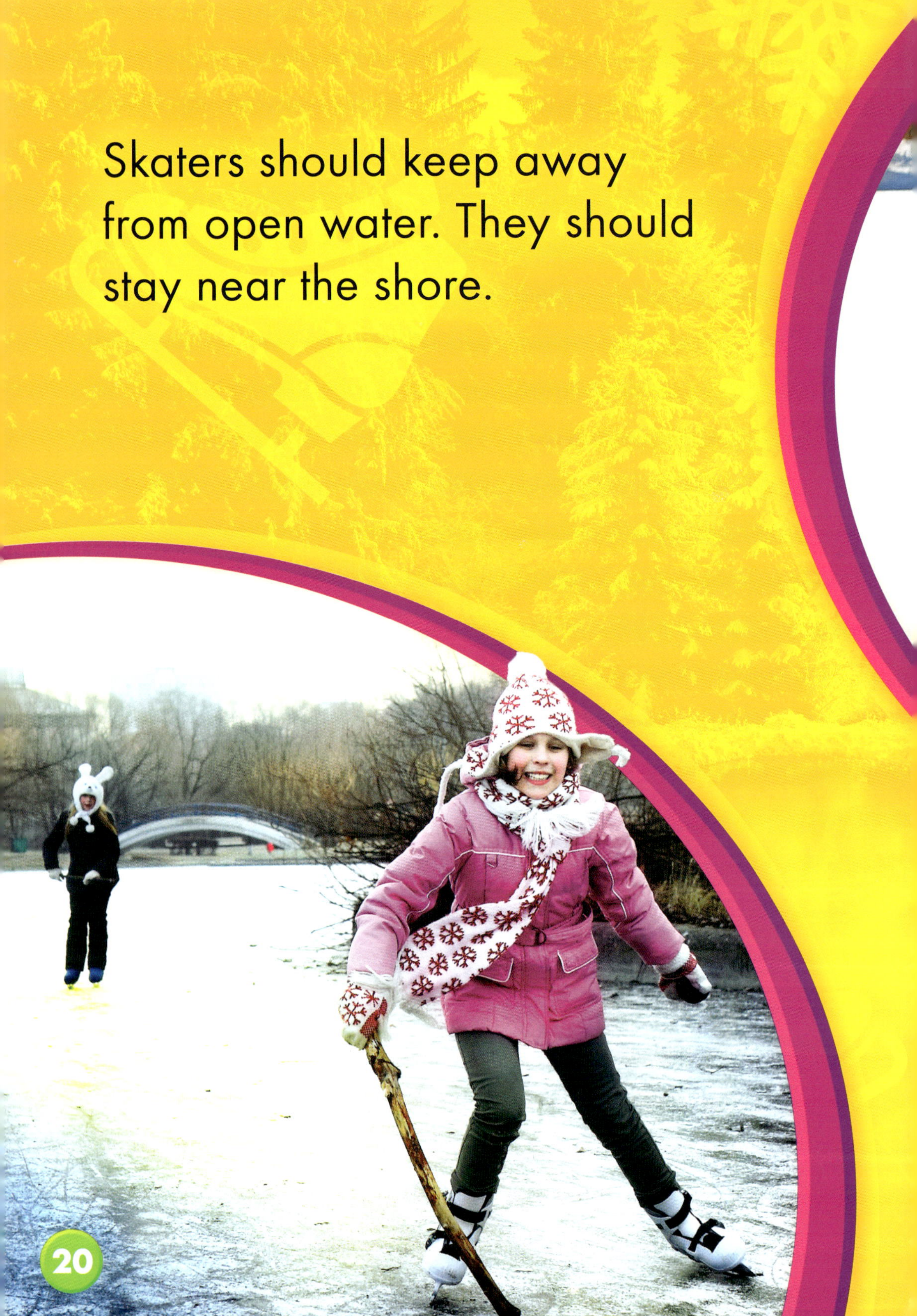

Skaters should keep away from open water. They should stay near the shore.

Skaters skate with a buddy. Friends make skating safe and fun!

Glossary

balance—to stay steady and not fall

figure skate—a kind of ice skating that includes jumps and spins

gliding—moving smoothly

ice picks—tools with sharp ends used for digging into ice

ice rinks—places with a sheet of ice, often with a wall built around it; ice rinks can be indoors or outdoors.

puck—a rubber disk used to play hockey

speed skate—a kind of ice skating in which skaters race against one another

toe picks—sawlike parts on the front of figure skates' blades that help skaters do tricks

To Learn More

AT THE LIBRARY

Fraser, Finley. *Winter Sports*. Minneapolis, Minn.: Bearport Publishing Company, 2022.

Gish, Ashley. *Figure Skating*. Mankato, Minn.: Creative Education, 2022.

Sherman, Jill. *Hockey*. Minneapolis, Minn.: Bellwether Media, 2020.

ON THE WEB

FACTSURFER

Factsurfer.com gives you a safe, fun way to find more information.

1. Go to www.factsurfer.com.
2. Enter "ice skating" into the search box and click 🔍.
3. Select your book cover to see a list of related content.

Index

The images in this book are reproduced through the courtesy of: Tatyana Vyc, front cover (hero); Victor Khymych, front cover (trees); Vikorya Telminova, front cover (frozen lake); FeelFree, p. 3; Neyman Kseniya, pp. 4-5; FatCamera, pp. 5, 6-7; BGSmith, p. 7; ingehogenbijl, p. 8; Maria Moroz, pp. 8-9; Galkin57, p. 10; Marina Korol, p. 11; John Danow, p. 11 (speed skating); Olga Besnard, pp. 12-13; Geofox, p. 12 (toe pick); Joseph Steven, p. 13 (figure skate); MCRMfotos, p. 13 (hockey skate); Real Sports Photos, p. 13 (speed skate); FamVeld, pp. 14-15; Lopolo, p. 15; Reimphoto, pp. 16-17; Jeppe Gustafsson/ Alamy, p. 17 (ice picks); Adam and Kev/ Getty Images, p. 18; Luboslav Ivanko, p. 19; Lapina, p. 20; ArtSvetlana, p. 21; NadyaEugene, p. 22.